HINDUISM
&
THE MODERN WORLD

HINDUISM
&
THE MODERN WORLD

BY

K. M. PANIKKAR

Foreign Minister of Patiala

GYAN

Published by

GYAN

Gyan Publishing House
5, Ansari Road
Daryaganj, New Delhi-110002
Phone: 011-47034999, 9811692060
E-mail: books@gyanbooks.com

Distribution Network
gyanbooks.com
India, USA, Canada, UK, Australia

ISBN: 978-81-212-8420-2 (HB)
First Published, 1938

2nd Impression 2024

Printed at: Gyan Press, Delhi.

HINDUISM & THE MODERN WORLD
Author: K. M. PANIKKAR

HINDUISM
&
THE MODERN WORLD

By

K. M. PANIKKAR

Foreign Minister of Patiala

KITABISTAN

ALLAHABAD

&

20-21, Tooks Court, LONDON, E. C. 4

CONTENTS

HINDUISM AND THE MODERN WORLD

CHAPTER I

INTRODUCTORY

The problem of the Hindu community has so far been treated as a national problem: that is one which exclusively affected the people of India. This is no doubt due to the national character of the religion which unlike Christianity, Islam and Buddhism, is confined, broadly speaking, to the geographical limits of India. The Christian religion extends to the four corners of the earth: Islam extends from Indonesia to Morocco and touches the life of European peoples at many points. Buddhism is equally an international factor. All questions affecting these religions are therefore not national but international. They are, in many cases, world-problems. The geographical limits of the Hindu religion and the fact that its effects do not extend to other nations, restrict the scope of the questions connected with Hinduism.

While this is undoubtedly true with regard to Hindu religion, can the same be said with regard to the peoples professing that religion? Humanity is indivisible and what affects 250 million people must necessarily be of interest and importance to the world as a whole. The position of the Hindus is a world problem. The religion of the Hindus may be their own concern: but it cannot be pretended that the weakness of the Hindu Race, which comprises of more than one-eighth of the population of the whole world is not a question which concerns others. The conception of humanity involves equally the conception that the progress of each section of it is a matter of importance for the whole. The world cannot therefore regard with indifference the conditions which prevent so large a portion of the world from making its legitimate contribution to the welfare of the whole. Modern social activity fully recognises this idea when it fights to abolish slavery in China, inhuman labour conditions in Congo and the exploitation of the Negro in Africa.

The loss to the world by the weakness of the Hindu people is undeniable. Their talents and gifts are undoubtedly great. Their contributions to the thought, to the material prosperity and to the artistic enjoyment of the world in the earlier periods of their history are proofs enough of the genius of the race. That so large a population should remain ineffective through preventible causes, should not make their legitimate contribution to the welfare of humanity, is a matter in which the rest of the world has a definite and inalienable interest.

The Hindu question is therefore a world problem. It may well be recognised that the other nations have from the beginning worked in unconscious realisation of this fact. The amazing missionary effort of the main European nations in India and to some extent of Islam is based on the recognition of the fact that the Hindu question is one which affects the whole world. Almost every country in Europe and the different churches of Christianity participate in the mission field. There is also the continuous conversion to Islam, no doubt less organised, but more effective in results. Though these activities are based on the realisation that the Hindu question is one which affects the whole world, there is a fundamental misconception which renders them futile. That is the belief that the reclamation of the Hindus and their rehabilitation in the world as an effective people is possible only through a change of religion, that it is the religion of the Hindus and not their social organisation and secular beliefs that stand in the way of their regeneration. They identify the Hindu religion with the social customs of the community and argue from that identification that conversion to other socio-religious organisations alone provides the way for Hindu regeneration. This unfortunate mixing up of religion with secular social organisation has had two results. It aroused all the powers of the Hindu religion in the defence of its social customs, as it made the Hindus believe that their customs, however unreasonable and however irreligious, are being attacked from a religious point of view. Secondly it made even internal reorganisation of Hindu society difficult as reformers came to be identified with the thought and practices of other religions.

The general body of Hindus had some justification in believing that the changes sought to be introduced into their secular customs really constituted a veiled attack on their religion. All the reform movements of the last century, it must be remembered, took as their basis the necessity of the purification of Hindu religion. The Brahmo Samaj, the Arya Samaj, the Prathana Samaj and other movements which started with the laudable object of reforming Hindu society confused the main issue and organised their movements on the basis of a *reform of religion.* It is the Christian missionary that inspired them, either by imitation as in the case of the Brahmo Samaj or through opposition as in the case of the Arya Samaj. The Hindu society as a result found its religion threatened from two sides, from the missionaries attacking it root and branch from outside and the Reformers attacking it from inside. The result was inevitable. The Hindu religion called forth all its powers to defend its institutions, right or wrong. Practices which had authority neither in religion nor in tradition came to be regarded as fundamental. Even the self-immolation of widows, never a widely prevalent practice, and one which certainly had no sanction in religion, began to find its defenders. It became impossible to bring reason to bear on social problems as the question of religion had become bound up with every aspect of Hindu life.

Also, there developed the protective argument of the Golden Age of Hinduism and the inadequacy of the "materialist" civilisation of the West. The myth of a Hindu Golden Age was both a reply to outside attack as well as a process of subconscious self-deception. It was a triumphant reply to the critic who accused Hinduism of being the cause of the degradation of the race. The Hindu was able to point out that his religion could not be the cause of the decay of the Hindu people, because in the great ages of the past when their ancestors founded empires, colonised distant countries and carried on the torch of science and civilisation, the same religion was professed by them. The most modern scientific inventions were seen into the past and the theory of "Hindu superiority" over the rest of mankind was advanced by serious thinkers. How far the so-called Golden Age has any historical basis we shall examine later. What is important here is to realise that the belief in a Golden Age is the characteristic of all decayed civilisations and is no more than the pathetic snobbishness of impoverished gentility which finds its mental sustenance and self-respect in a glorious and often fictitious past. The fact however is forgotten that if there was a comparatively glorious past, that would provide no justification for continuing in the present degradation. The past as an inspiration for the present and the future is undoubtedly of importance: but a past however great which instead of inspiring the present for greater achievements only provides an excuse for shutting one's eye to progress is worse than having no history at all.

The idea of a "materialistic West" is equally a self-deception. Society is indeed a secular organisation and must inevitably be governed by material considerations. Even assuming that India is spiritual, which as I shall attempt to demonstrate is in itself a false notion, the organisation of mundane affairs and their regulation in a society postulates not spiritual but materialistic values. The organisation of human life, the distribution of wealth, the corporate activity of people for the betterment of the physical basis of living—these are not affairs of spirit but of matter. It is the material conception of life which should govern these factors. It is no argument to say that as spirit is more important than matter, it is sufficient for men to be concerned with affairs of the spirit and they can leave affairs of matter alone. Whether Hindu society gives that importance to affairs of spirit or whether it is in any way more "spiritual" than the West is also a matter for enquiry.

On what is India's claim to be more spiritual than the West based? Is it on the ground that her thinkers in the past devoted themselves to metaphysical enquiries rather than to the better ordering of the world; or on the ground that the ideal they enunciated attached greater importance to ethical and moral things than to worldly prosperity; or that greatness in the world in India was measured not by worldly achievement but by spiritual attainment? On any of these grounds the claim that India is spiritual and that Europe is materialistic seems to be totally unsustainable. Even assuming that the vedic *rishis* and seers of the Upanishads had greater spiritual attainment and the store of wisdom accumulated in India in these matters is greater than in Europe, the essential question to be faced is how far have the masses in India inherited this wisdom and guided their life according to the teachings of those *rishis* and seers. How far in fact has the spirit of Hindu philosophy —assuming that its teachings are more spiritual—permeated the masses? India can have no national claim to that thought unless it is translated in her national life. And can it be maintained that now or at any other time in the past Indian society was organised on the basis of the wisdom of the Vedas and the Upanishads any more than the life in Europe has been organised on the basis of Christian teaching. If thought, apart from activity be the guide, then Europe should be considered equally spiritual. But, it may be argued, that Europe in pursuit of material happiness does not live up to Christian ideals. The reply is, does India live up to its spiritual ideals? Steeped in superstition, governed in their religious life by usages and customs which are both irrational and irreligious, do the preponderant majority of Hindus know even what these ideals are? The spiritual life of India in practice is no more than a degraded and meaningless affectation of religiosity, a mere adherence to forms the meaning of which is utterly lost to the many. Any serious study of European life would on the other hand convince the enquirer that side by side with the grossest materialism, with the brazen worship of the mammon—which is by no means less prevalent in India—there exist in Europe a spirit of disciplined service, a desire for the well being of mankind as such, a deep sensitiveness to suffering and misery born of a profound humanism which constitute a unique translation of the religion of the spirit in practical life. There may be much to say against organised churches, about their complacency, about their worldliness, about their acceptance of the evils of the world. But is the position of the Mahants, Jagatgurus, and the heads of religious orders any better in India? On the other hand in Europe, outside the organised machinery of the churches and to a less degree even inside them, there is an undoubted mass of selfless activity—disciplined, directed and purposeful—for the moral welfare of the world. Has present-day "spiritual" India anything to compare with the great Orders of the Catholic Church—men and women recruited from all classes of society, vowed to chastity, poverty and hard life—who are spread in the different corners of the world dedicating their life to the service of fellow men? Has India anything to compare with the beneficent activity of lay societies in European countries which found hospitals, fight epidemics and other scourges like leprosy, tuberculosis and cancer? Could these selfless activities—voluntary, enthusiastic, and continuous—be carried on by people who are materialistic and alleged to be pursuing their own individual happiness? The Hindus proudly proclaim that their national ideal is *Nishkama Karma* —service without reward. May be: Krishna has undoubtedly preached it in the Gita. But apart from individuals, has any section of Hindu society practised that ideal? How do the theoretical followers of *Nishkama Karma* compare in selfless activity with the materialists of Europe? Whatever selfless social activity there is in India today is the outcome of the inspiration of Western practice. The organisation of the Ramakrishna mission for example is frankly based on the monastic orders of Christianity; the Arya mission on missionary societies: the Seva Samiti on boy scouts etc. It is true that in most cases the Western wine was poured into Indian bottles as when Swami Vivekananda kept the form of the orthodox Sanyasins though organising his Order on the ideals of service of Western monastic organisations.

A further important point which may be emphasised here and which has had disastrous results on the thought of Hindus and Europeans is the artificial division between the East and the West. This false division had its origin in the feeling of superiority which Europeans through their political power came to have in Asia. The European claimed superiority for everything which emanated from the West and in popular thought the West came to stand for progress and the East for retrogression. It was forgotten that progress at no time was the monopoly of any particular geographical area and that in the East itself there were different nations whose attitude towards life was not always reactionary. The important point for us is that an artificial division came to be accepted in popular thought and as a consequence it became almost a dogmatic belief that rival theories of life were standing in opposition to each other. This conception was popularised by a school of historians who in their supreme faith in the inherent greatness of everything European conceived even history as an epic battle between the Western *suras* and the Eastern *asuras*, forces of light and darkness, struggling for the mastery of the human soul. The battle of Salamis is supposed to have saved civilisation. The conquest of Spain by the Moors and the defeat of the Crusaders are supposed to have been a victory for the forces of darkness while the battle of Lepanto was again the saving of civilisation. Leo the Isaurian "saved civilisation" according to Herbert Fisher: Charles Martel saved it again at Poiters. According to this school of history there is a permanent and standing conspiracy against civilisation by the people of the East and every victory of Europe even when it is by the barbarian Franks against the Moors is a victory for civilisation.

This idea of an epic conflict between the East and the West, spurious as a historical conception and meaningless in its view of humanity, has had the result of putting the East in an attitude of defence in regard to its own philosophy of life as against the philosophy, the knowledge and the social organisation of Europe. It encouraged the belief that the Eastern view was something different, which though temporarily defeated would in due course assert itself. It prevented the Oriental nations from examining the social conceptions and the moral ideas of the Europeans in an independent and objective manner, exactly as it led the European nations to brush aside contemptuously as inferior everything which came from the East. The conception of an indivisible humanity which grows by the co-ordination of the thought of different people and by the synthesis of regional cultures was obscured by this artificial distinction which created the fear of Europe in the minds of Hindus and the contempt of Hindus in the minds of Europeans.

The attack on religion has now definitely failed. The missionaries have no longer any hope of converting the whole of India to Christianity. Equally decisive has been the failure of the movements which desired a reform of religion. The Brahmo Samaj, though its influence with educated Hindus in Bengal is still considerable, has as a religion sunk into a minor sect. The Arya Samaj has also lost its momentum and is important only as a militant section of Hinduism, anxious to vindicate the truth of vedic revelation. The hope that the Hindu people could be reformed and Hindu society reorganised through a religious reformation has altogether vanished. The Hindu question remains where it was, except that it has now come to be widely recognised that its solution cannot be through the machinery of religion. It is not the Hindu religion that is at fault. It is not Hindu religion that requires to be reorganised. It is Hindu Society. The distinction is fundamental and the failure of all movements so far has arisen from the fact that this essential point had been overlooked. As Hinduism never produced an organised church, it has remained a matter of personal faith. It has no set of dogmas, no orthodox or accepted tradition, no books except the *vedas* whose validity cannot be denied. Religion with the Hindus is a matter of personal faith and individual practices. No doubt the practices are to a large extent guided by recognised caste traditions, but it has to be remembered that neither the denial of the validity of those traditions, nor the refusal to follow those practices affect the religious orthodoxy of a Hindu. As a result, social organisation is essentially unconnected with religion, though through historical reasons, as we shall try to show, it came to be identified with religion. The re-organisation of society has therefore to be undertaken independently of religion and entirely as a secular matter.

The problem may briefly be stated as follows: How can the Hindus be made vigorous, active and healthy members, instead of being the invalids as they are now, of the Human Family. What National *Risorgimento* can convert the helpless millions whose contribution to human welfare is nil today and who keep alive on the intellectual charity of others, into partners in the world Civilisation. It is obvious that constituted as the Hindus are, they are in no position to participate effectively in the shaping of human destiny. Before the Hindus can take their place with the civilised peoples, it is necessary that they should bring their society in line with modern ideas and purge themselves of the numerous weaknesses which render them ineffective in every aspect of life. The importance of this problem has long been recognised by thinkers in India. It is the realisation of this fact that led to the various Reform movements in an earlier generation. Their failure makes it necessary to re-examine the whole question and to discover other and better methods for the reconstruction of Hindu life.

The thesis which it is sought to establish may also be stated here. The argument of this book would be to prove :

(1) That the social organisation of Hinduism is the result of unregulated growth, which through historical reasons has been stunted in its early stages.

(2) The fragmentisation of social feeling is its essential characteristic and this fragmentisation is based on the twin institutions of family and caste.

(3) That the institutions of the Hindu peoples are unconnected with their religion and are based entirely on law and custom and are therefore secular.

(4) That, being secular and based on law and custom they require continuous re-examination and modification through legislation.

It is further the basic argument of this book that the degeneration of the Hindu people is due to the prolonged absence of legislative authority following on the breakdown of the political power of Hinduism: that the co-existence of a society organised on the basis of a Revealed Law—Islam—and the failure of Hindus to create within their own society an authority to which social obedience is due have led to a crystallisation of institutions and customs which by analogy came to be considered sacred by each group into which the society was divided. On the basis of these arguments, it is sought to prove that the survival of the Hindu peoples is dependent on their organisation into a community through national legislation which will re-emphasise the secular character of Hindu organisations and sweep away the dead customs which through misunderstanding have come to be identified with their religion.

The problem facing the Hindus may therefore be formulated as a rethinking of social values, a re-organisation of social institutions and a divorce between law and custom on the one hand and religion on the other. This threefold problem is interconnected because the orthodox section of Hindus holds that every institution however abhorrent to humanity (like untouchability) however unreasonable (like caste) and however anachronistic (like the Joint Family) has the implicit sanction of religion and cannot be touched by secular legislation without offending the religious susceptibilities of the Hindus. We shall show that this claim is totally baseless. Indeed if it had any truth, the Hindu community would have no claim to share in the political power of the State. But such a claim fortunately has never found acceptance even among the Hindus. The more intelligent among them have during the last 100 years vigorously rejected these obscurantist pretensions and have at least since the time of Rammohan Roy in the early years of the 19th century increasingly asserted the right and duty of the state to change social institutions and customs by secular legislation.

CHAPTER II

THE SOCIAL STRUCTURE OF HINDUISM

The Hindu social structure revolves round two fundamental institutions; the Caste and the Joint family. Everything connected with the Hindu people, outside their religion, can be traced to these two institutions. These in fact are the differentiating characteristics of Hindu life. Now what is caste? The ideal view is that Hindu society is divided into four castes, the Brahmins or the priestly class, the Kshatriyas or the fighting class, Vaisyas or the trading class and Sudras the working class. Now it would be obvious even on a casual examination that this fourfold division is only ideological and not in any manner based on fact. It is, as we propose to show, only an ex-post facto systematisation on a horizontal basis. It is what the Hindu sociologists desired their society to be, a theory of caste-idealism based on the fundamental functions of life. That the fourfold functions never existed in fact can be historically proved. True, the Brahmins as a caste separated themselves with the development of ritual in Hinduism and they can be said to be the only integrated caste in Hindu society. But even among them, though a general feeling of Brahminhood existed and exists, there are today no less than 1,800 main sub-castes, and perhaps many thousand more whose gradations cannot properly be traced. When there are 1800 sub-castes in Brahmins themselves, each of which claims superiority over the other, the idea of the unity of the Brahmin caste vanishes utterly. But the Brahmins are a caste—all other castes recognise them to be so. They have a common body of religious rites, and broadly speaking a common attitude towards life. But where are the other three castes? Who is the Kshatriya? The only answer possible is that a Kshatriya is one who belongs to any group of families who claim to be Kshatriyas. The Rajputs who are said to be Kshatriyas *par excellence* are themselves communities whose origin is mysterious and who came to be known to history only after the 8th century. The great royal families, of whom we have record, were none of them Kshatriyas. The Mauryas—the first imperial dynasty whose achievements are known to us—were Sudras. The

Vakatakas and Barasivas were Brahmins: the Guptas were Jats. The Thaneswas dynasty belonged to the Vaisya Caste.[1] Where did the Kshatriya community disappear in the thousand years between Chandra Gupta Maurya 320 B.C., and Harsha Vardhana? (637 A.D.)

Today, apart from Ruling families who claim to be Kshatriyas on the basis of their function of Rulership, where is the great caste which is said to be one of the fourfold divisions of Hinduism? Any group of families or of sub-castes which desires to rise in the social grade claims Kshatriyahood. The Kayasthas of North India, a highly educated and powerful community, have announced their intention of regarding themselves as Kshatriyas. The Vaisya caste is equally a non-existent generalisation.

The fact is that the fourfold castes were merely a theoretical division of society to which the tribes and the family groups were affiliated. The census today gives the names of more than 3,000 castes, with innumerable subdivisions among them. The fourfold division is therefore merely a fiction—a

[1] See "Origin and development of Hindu Kingship" by the present writer.

platonic myth.

But though the four castes exist only in idea, the theory of society based on them still governs Hindu life. Every one of the innumerable sub-castes claims to belong to one of the four. They are all theoretically within the fold of the main ideological Castes. The principles of this caste division are therefore of the utmost importance. The ideas of caste rule Hindu life. Its non-realisation in institutions is from the point of view of its evil effects unimportant.

The essential principles of caste are:

(1) unchangeable inequality based on birth,
(2) the gradation of professions and their inequality, and
(3) restrictions on marriage outside one's own group.[1]

A man's caste is decided by his birth. From one caste to another there is no passage. If a man is born a Sudra, he remains all his life a Sudra: he must marry only a Sudra and according to caste-theory can only carry on the professions allotted to the Sudra. How the Brahmin theorists justified

[1] For a discussion of these three principles, see the author's Caste and Democracy. (Hogarth Press)

the establishment of a society based on irremovable inequality under which the vast majority of population was forced to accept the stigma of inferiority need not be discussed here. It constitutes a most interesting example of the overwhelming influence of institutions on the mind of man.

It is however necessary to add that while the inequality of birth and the prohibitions in regard to marriage continue with undiminished force, the attempt to confine castes to separate professions seems never to have succeeded. The earliest available literature gives instances of Brahmins carrying on the profession of medicine and arms and administration. In the Jatakas the Brahmins are mentioned as traders, hunters and trappers. Masani quotes the case of a Kshatriya prince, Kusa, mentioned in Jataka tales who became an apprentice by turn under a potter, basket-maker, florist and cook. Conversely there have been from the earliest days innumerable cases of men of the lowest position in caste-society, attaining high rank. We have already mentioned the case of the Maurya Emperors. Even today a large number of the Ruling Families in India belong to aboriginal castes, though many have assumed Kshatriahood, or at least put forward claims to belong to a higher caste.

Obviously therefore, except as an ideological division, the fourfold caste had no existence. What had existence and mattered much more than the ideal division into four castes, were the innumerable sub-castes, each divided into smaller units. The three thousand major units of caste enumerated in census returns constitute a factor of supreme importance. These castes are rigidly exclusive and each is independent of the other. Neither inter-marriage nor inter-dining between them is permitted. They are aliens to each other in social life.

This is fragmentisation with a vengeance. The operation of the system of caste divides up Hindu peoples into such small units as to render the development of any common social feeling impossible. The influence of this fragmentisation has elsewhere been described by me in the following words:

"The passage from the barbarous to the civilised state of existence has been marked everywhere by an extension of the circle of social activity or in the words of Durkheim by the widening of "the symbiotic circle". In primitive societies the individual stands related either to the family or to the tribe which is only family on a totemic basis. The progress of human civilisation is based on the extension of the principle of thought and activity. Though indubitably this is the universal rule, in India after the society passed through its early stages of civilisation, the process was soon revised. The symbiotic circle instead of being widened was continuously narrowed by a system of marriage regulations. The wider social activity of the individual found no scope. The collective consciousness of social life which is the creative force of civilising activity and is therefore responsible for the highest forms of social endeavour tended to vanish as the marriage restrictions developed more and more."

If the castes had integrated into the more ideological divisions that the Chātruvarnya (the four-fold) ideal conceived, this fragmentisation of society would never have happened. The four castes would have meant a simplification of the chaos, the evolution of a general system of order out of the confusing and tragic anarchy which the process of division produced. The conception of the four castes involved the conception of *a community*. It was the organisation of the people on certain understandable lines. The grim tragedy however is that even this amount of integration was absent in India and the theory of the four castes remained no more than an ideal.

All the attempted justification of caste has been of the fourfold division. *But even that system has no religious sanction of any kind.* As a recent author points out :

"The seers of the early vedic period know nothing of caste. Delve as much as one may into the literature of the period, one discovers only classes, not castes. The elements which go to form castes were however there so that gradually a gulf was created between one order and another. For a long time however the conception of social segregation and untouchability was repugnant to the genius of the people who sought unity in variety and dissolved variety in unity. Each class was regarded as an integral part of the fabric of society."[1]

In fact caste as a social crystallisation is invariably *a late development in a decaying civilisation.* Splengler in his celebrated book 'The Decline of the West' analyses the phenomenon as follows: "The distinction between Estate and Caste is that bet-

[1] 'Caste and the structure of society', by R. P. Masani—Legacy of India, p. 132.

ween earliest culture and latest civilisation. In the rise of the prime Estates—noble and priest—the culture is unfolding itself, while the castes are the expression of its definitive fellah-state. The Estate is the most living of all culture launched on the path of fulfilment, "the form that living must itself unfold". The caste is absolute finishedness, the phase in which development has been succeeded by immutable fixation."[1]

If the Vedas provide no authority for the caste system in what way is it connected with religion? It is true all Hindu law takes caste for granted; all the puranas assume the existence of caste and look upon it as divinely ordained. But where is the authority for this theory of the Divine ordinance of caste? True, the *Gita* declares: "Chāturvarnyam mayā sristạm Gunakarma vibhāgaçah", but clearly that statement of Sri Krishna is an attack on the basis of Hindu caste-system and not its justification. The literal meaning of Krishna's words is, "I created the fourfold society *on the basis of quality and action.*" It is the most unequivocal repudiation of the divine origin of caste system based on birth: the most categorical denial of the Brahminical

[1] Splengler's 'Decline of the West', Vol. II, p. 333.

claims of inherent superiority. No one denies that even in "classless" societies, life has to be organised on the basis of *guna* (quality) and *Karma* (action), but the idea that Hindu religion gives sanction to inequality based on birth seems to be untrue on the face of this statement in the most sacred of all Hindu texts outside the Vedas: and the Vedas as we have seen give no justification to the theory either.

If religion does not, what gives the appearance of religious sanction to the caste-system? The answer is *Hindu Law*. Manu undoubtedly bases his whole code on caste-system. But no divine character was claimed, as I shall try to show, for Manu's laws by the Brahmins themselves till comparatively recent times. In fact a historical enquiry into the origin of Hindu codes would clearly establish that they grew but slowly and were never in the days of their formation considered unchangeable or divinely inspired.

Another significant fact which may be emphasised here is that though Manu and the law-givers assume the existence of four castes it is obvious from their texts that even at that time, the fourfold division was merely ideological and the social facts of innumerable sub-castes intruded inescapably into their calculations.

Therefore, even if we accept that the fourfold division is ordained by God, the Hindu caste-system which from its earliest days was not a system of four castes, but of innumerable sub-castes each segregated from the other, cannot claim any religious sanction. It is essentially a social growth—the result of the anarchy of Hindu social life. This society of sub-castes is so closely connected with and dependent upon that other characteristic organisation of the Hindus, the joint family, that it is to this institution we must now turn to understand the full significance of its disintegrating influence.

These two institutions, the caste and the joint family, though in theory unconnected, are in practice interlocked to an extent which makes them in effect a single institution. The unit of the Hindu community is not the individual, but the joint family. Its widest expression is the "sub-caste", which consists of a few joint families which are permitted to "inter-marry" and "inter-dine". Beyond this extended joint family, the Hindu theorists recognised no society or community. That is the widest social group the Hindus evolved. The joint family is, therefore, the rock on which the Hindu social organisation is built. The modern pseudo-sociologists of India have claimed many virtues for it and some Hindu and non-Hindu writers have seen in it the essence of Hindu culture. They argue that the joint family suppresses the selfishness of individualism, by regulating rigidly the conduct of individuals in relation to a wider community: that it modifies the evils of private property, by vesting proprietorship in a group: that it renders the essential social services, such as old age pension, unemployment insurance, etc., to the importance of which Europe has awakened only recently and so on. It is unnecessary to go into these arguments. Every primitive institution is based on communal welfare. The whole theory of primitive tribalism is that: but it cannot therefore be argued that it is better to live in a State of totemic tribalism than to evolve higher social organisations.

The joint family is nothing more than the survival of the primitive familial community, which before the conception of society had dawned on man, created around itself walls of blood relationship and economic identity. It subordinated the individual to the group (family), provided him with a code of morals, with duties and obligations and modified his "enlightened selfishness" by the ties of the family. That it was a great step from primitive life to civilisation would easily be conceded.

It provided an organised life, by establishing a principle of social obedience. At all times, the central difficulty of civilisation has been the establishment of a principle of obedience receiving universal acceptance as just and natural and to which the people will subordinate their wills. In primitive and "savage" communities, this was provided by the loyalty to the tribe which was enforced by *tabus* and *manas*. But it is essential to remember that the Totemic tribe is a family united together in blood relationship with the totem. Thus the members of the Eagle tribe are blood relations through the common ancestor. As Longfellow says in the *Hiawatha*:

From what ancestral totem
Be it eagle, bear or beaver
They descended, this we know not.

No doubt the relationship is fictitious but the important point is that the primitive mind could trace the principles of loyalty and obedience only through blood.

The change from the fictitious family to the real family as the unit is an important one in social growth. The patriarchal (or the matriarchal) family in which the pater-familias is the undisputed master and exacts obedience from the rest is a known stage in the history of civilisation. But outside India, in time it led to a further broadening of the social bases, mainly by two processes; first, by the limitation of the family from the wide community of all blood relations that it originally was, to the strictly individualistic conception of it; and secondly, by the gradual evolution of a conception of obligations and duties, transcending the family and extending to the whole community. In India the system of the joint family not only persisted but grew in strength as a result of the absence of these two processes. The absence of a unified secular authority to suit legislation to social needs tended to crystallise customs and strengthen institutions which had the blessings of old-law givers. The laws of the Hindus came to be mixed up with the religion. They were "revealed" codes. The fact that the Hindus had neither a supreme pontiff nor a curia made it worse as there was no religious authority competent to change the *Smiritis.* Neither State nor Church existed and the result was that institutions which had the authority of the ancient law-givers could not be changed except by Desāchāra or Kulāchāra, that is local or family customs.

What has been the effect of this two-faced institution, the caste and the joint family, on the Hindu peoples? Primarily it subdivides continuously the social organism that the units become microscopic and unrelated to society. Thus it denies the entire theory of *community*, and bases the organisation of Hindu life on the opposite principle of disintegration and division. From its point of view the Hindus are no more than an inchoate mass of small units unrelated to each other. Secondly, it enshrines and upholds the principle of *inequality*, as each sub-caste considers itself superior to most if not to all others. No organisation of society on the basis of equality is possible as long as the sub-caste and the joint family exist. Thirdly, it bases itself and in consequence emphasises at every turn the principle of segregation and exclusiveness. The sub-caste ceases to exist if inter-marriage and inter-dining are permitted between them. Naturally, therefore, the whole power of the institution is turned against any attempt to break down the restrictions of food and marriage. No wonder that Tagore is moved to speak of Hindu social organisations as walls which shut out "the sunshine of thought and the breath of life" and an outside observer, to speak in terms of bitterness as follows:

"The high metaphysics of the Upanishads and the ethics of the Gita have been reduced to mere words by the tyranny of caste. Emphasising the unity of the whole world animate and inanimate India has, yet fostered a social system which has divided her children into watertight compartments, divided them from one another generation to generation for endless centuries. It has exposed her to foreign conquests which have left her poor and weak and worst of all she has become the home of untouchability and unapproachability which have branded her with the curse of Cain."[1]

There can be no denying that the organisation of Hindu life on the basis of the sub-caste and the joint family extinguishes the social sense as the feeling of obligation *to a social whole* and thereby renders the conception of a unified Hindu society impossible. It is not Hindu religion that has branded India with the curse of Cain but Hindu law, and the meetings of untouchables who in their processions burn the Code of Manu show a greater appreciation of the fundamental factors of this

[1] Prof. Wadia, 'Contemporary Indian Philosophy', p. 368.

problem than the philosophers and sociologists who try to justify caste.

CHAPTER III

THE THREAT OF THE HARIJANS

The elementary facts about untouchability may be summarised as follows. Spread all over India there are over 60 million people, divided into different castes, tribes and sub-castes, who by their mere touch and in some cases even their shadow pollute others. How far this is carried is best illustrated from the practice in Malabar, the unpolluted sanctuary of orthodoxy, where there is a graded system of distances for castes, nearer than which their approach pollutes the members of a superior caste. Till recently such castes were not permitted to use even the same roads. They could not bathe in the same tanks, draw water from the same well, attend the same schools. In other parts of India though there is no distance-pollution, the untouchable castes are not permitted to draw water from the same well, attend the same schools and, of course, they could not worship in the temple without polluting God himself. These customs mean in the first place a denial of opportunities so complete as to keep the untouchables perpetually in a state of serfdom. In the second place they mean an absolute segregation, an exclusion from all contact such as no community was ever able to enforce anywhere else in the world.

Through the activities of Christian missionaries and of Mahommedan conversions the untouchables awoke after the sleep of thousands of years to their elementary human *rights*. The Christian government of India insisted that, whatever the custom of the Hindus, once an untouchable becomes a Christian no *humiliating* restrictions could be put on him. In Travancore in the time of Dalhousie, they threatened the Maharaja with deposition, because a converted untouchable had been assaulted while trying to force his entry into a caste Hindu's house. In the result the untouchables who accepted Christianity came to possess higher social rank. The effect of this was not lost on these communities. In many places a good many of them became Christians and others who remained Hindus began to clamour for social equality.

The effect of Islam was more pronounced. While the racial aspect of Christianity in India, being mainly a *religion* of the Europeans, tended to revive some of the features of caste among the Christian converts, Islam with its vigorous democratic conception, put down all such differences among its converts. During the days when Muslims ruled North India, the Hindu community as it was self-governing in its internal affairs was able to maintain its hold on the untouchables. The influence of Islam was felt mainly through reform movements like those of Kabir and Nanak. But in recent times Islam came prominently into the field as a rival of Christianity for the organised conversion of the untouchables. The untouchable communities found themselves courted and flattered and the attractions of rival religions held up to them. The Hindus also awoke to the danger that faced them. Till 1920—the arrival of Gandhiji in Indian politics—untouchability had been looked upon by the Hindus as a social problem. Mr. Gandhiji realised that it was the great political problem of the future: the emergence of the sixty million toilers from their degraded position into full citizenship. The non-cooperation movement put the eradication of untouchability in the front of its programme. Everywhere the Congress took it up as a part of their political work.

Along with this, the influence of the Montagu-

Chelmsford Reforms has also to be taken into consideration. The partial democracy of that constitution gave to the untouchables in the provinces considerable voting power. Orthodox high caste men had to canvass their votes in order to get elected. As a result the last fifteen years have witnessed a remarkable revolution in the attitude of the main body of Hindus to this question. The untouchables themselves have been organised into effective political parties, under capable leadership. With political organisation a new sense of self-respect has come which has shown itself in a hundred different ways. Their record of activity has also been remarkable. The ten years from the Vaikam Satyagraha (Civil Disobedience) in 1924-25, for the purpose of securing the right to use public roads to the crisis that led to the announcement by Dr. Ambedkar in 1935 that if the Hindus did not accept their claims, large bodies of untouchables would choose some other religion, have been a period of intense activity which has covered centuries in one leap. In Travancore all temples have been thrown open to them. In Madras, the Government is sponsoring a bill for the removal of all disabilities under which they have so long laboured. Even the Hindu Mahasabha—the organisation of orthodox Hindus—is stirring itself to secure for these castes rights which social custom had denied to them for centuries.

The Brahmin apologists of caste who from the pinnacle of their philosophical wisdom beguile themselves and try to beguile others that it is to the undoubted good of the world that society should be organised horizontally, with themselves of course at the top, and claim that caste is the great achievement of the Hindu genius for synthesis conveniently forget these sixty million untouchables who constitute the submerged basis of the Hindu pyramid. Sir S. Radhakrishnan sees in untouchability the humanity of the higher castes who in their recognition of the philosophic truth "that the savage and the primitive, the barbarous and the backward.....also in their imperfect fashions are struggling towards that abiding city which shines in dazzling splendour up the steep and narrow way"[1] let them live instead of trying to annihilate them as other conquering nations did. He adds :—
"In dealing with the problem of the conflict of the different social groups, Hinduism adopted the only safe course of democracy viz., that each racial

[1] Hindu View of life, p. 95.

group should be allowed to develop the best in it without impeding the progress of others."[1] Philosophy may be speculative and mere words may satisfy the philosophical enquirer. Laymen have no method of judging questions of philosophical validity. But when philosophers try to explain the facts of social life all their words can have meaning only if they are related to the inescapable facts of life. They cannot take shelter behind texts and theories of appearances and reality. What are the facts of untouchability? Does Sir S. Radhakrishnan claim that the communities classed as untouchables were left free to develop themselves to their full mental stature, now or at any historical time? Is it an evidence of that freedom that the customs of untouchability and even approachability were enforced against them; that education was denied to them, that no mantra, no initiation was open to them; that they were not allowed to use the same roads which dogs and unclean animals were permitted to use, to draw water from the same wells, not to worship even at the temples. Indeed a very philosophical method of developing their individuality. Perhaps it is

[1] Hindu View of life, p. 97.

also an evidence of this scheme of allowing them to reach "the abiding city which shines in dazzling splendour" that they were permitted to live segregated in unclean areas, away from the dwellings of civilised men, that the social codes punished with all the rigour of their barbarous cruelty any attempt of the untouchables to elevate themselves either by education or by a change of occupation or of the conditions of livelihood. Sir S. Radhakrishnan cannot argue that it is only "now" that the Hindu "synthesis" has become an instrument of oppression. The facts of history stand out only too clearly on this matter. It is after all only *now*—after 2,500 years of oppression—that the untouchables' position is getting slowly improved. The idea that untouchability was a fall from the pristine purity of the Brahmin synthesis could hardly be put forward.

The fact is that untouchability is not the result of any synthesis at all. The untouchables were not a "problem" for the Hindu sociologist. They were the *avarnas*, the non-caste men, communities outside the pale of Hindu social organisation. It was in no philosophic conception of allowing them to develop their own life that the Hindus declined to bring these people within their social body. Their attitude towards the untouchable was infinitely worse than that of the master to slave. The slave at least was a chattel of the master: he stood in an individual relation to his owner. Considerations of economic self-interest and even human feelings modified the barbarism of personal slavery. But even these mitigating factors did not apply to the system of untouchability.

Untouchability, if closely examined, would be seen to be a system of *communal slave holding*. Instead of individuals owning slaves, each village held the untouchable families attached to it in a communal slavery. No personal or social considerations were permitted in the least degree to modify the rigour of the system. No individual had any personal relations with an untouchable. Custom provided what the functions of the untouchables were in relation to the village. Socially, economically and even from the point of view of law, Hindu society kept down the untouchables with all the strength of its iron hand.

At least in this matter the influence of the British Government and more especially of English law, has been on the side of social justice. The total displacement of the criminal law of the Hindus annihilated at one stroke the legal sanction of the principle of inequality. The Indian Penal Code insists on the equality of all men before law and the punishment awarded to a Brahmin for killing an untouchable is, strange and perverse as it may seem to Hindu philosophers, the same as to an untouchable killing a Brahmin. The legal background of untouchability has gone, never to come back. The social disabilities are more difficult to remove. But even here the activities of the British Government perhaps incidentally, have effected changes the importance of which is only being realised now.

The apologists of caste fall in two categories: Brahmin sophists like Sir S. Radhakrishnan who, as becomes a philosopher, discourses on the ideal view of caste, of the division into four varnas and justifies it on the ground that "it illustrates the spirit of comprehensive synthesis characteristic of the Hindu mind with its faith in the collaboration of races and the co-operation of cultures:"[1] and secondly, Hindus as well as non-Hindus who admire the powers of resistance to outside influence which the institution of caste has shown through centuries. Of this class of writers the late Mr.

[1] Hindu View of life, p. 93.

K. T. Paul,[1] the most distinguished thinker that the Indian Christian community has produced may be taken as an example. Mr. Paul's view is: 'so subtle and intangible as scarcely to reveal its power over its own members so long as there is no transgression, the Hindu social system has been through the centuries the most potent in holding every individual to his social obligations, religious duties as also to his economic and civic responsibilities. To it is due the perfection in craftsmanship brought about by a process of apprenticeship from father to son through perhaps two hundred generations. To it is due the protection of the widow and the orphan, the aged and the infirm, the under-privileged and the handicapped. To it is also due the steady pursuit of knowledge and culture through these classes who were, so to say, told off to devote themselves exclusively to it as students and teachers. Caste has large dark blots in its scheme and is today happily undermined to its foundations. But India owes all that is her distinctive identity almost exclusively to the protection afforded by caste and by its unchallengeable potentiality for good."

The Brahmin apologist uses all the casuistry

[1] Paul, 'British connection with India', S.C.M., p. 37.

of his language to justify an institution which historically never existed and to give it high moral and ethical purpose. He postulates an ideal theory of caste which he justifies on ethical and moral grounds while condemning vigorously its practical effects. "Though it has *now* degenerated," says Sir S. Radhakrishnan "into *an instrument of oppression and intolerance* and though it tends to perpetuate inequality and develop the spirit of exclusiveness, these unfortunate effects are not the central motives of the system." The philosopher gives up his case to begin with on the practical effects of caste to-day. He agrees that the system today is an instrument of oppression and intolerance: that it perpetuates inequality and develops exclusiveness. But presumably he holds that at one time it did not. The question for examination therefore is, *at what stage in the history of caste was it not an instrument of oppression and of intolerance*. Was it in Buddha's time, in the Mauryan Era, in the Gupta period, or in any other of the known ages of Indian history, or merely in an ideal age postulated by philosophers? In all the known periods of Indian history after the system of caste had come into existence, it has been an instrument of intolerance and oppression. In the time of King Rama of the Ramayana we know that the Brahmins complained against the austerities of a sudra sanyasi and Rama is praised for having killed him for the heinous crime of being religious! In the Buddha's time the intolerance of caste was such that the Thathagata raised his voice most strongly against it. The Arthasastra provides sufficient evidence of the system of caste being used as an instrument of oppression. Sir S. Radhakrishnan's attempt at justifying caste by declaring its present injustices as being due to degeneration and by appealing to an age when caste in its purity was an illustration of the comprehensive synthesis of which the Hindu mind was capable, is therefore both unhistorical and meaningless. It is in no way related to the caste system as practised at any time and it is no argument merely to quote texts to show that caste was tolerant when practice was far from justifying the theories which modern apologists desire to read into stray texts.

With much of what Mr. Paul says no one could disagree. The powers of resistance which the caste system has displayed have been really unique. But such powers were against States which had either no legislative power like the Musalman kingdoms, or did not use them as in the case of the British. Undoubtedly the system of hereditary occupation which underlies the economic conception of caste led to perfection of craftsmanship. But at what price was the perfection of craftsmanship bought: by keeping the vast body of Hindus submerged in superstition and ignorance, and Mr. Paul himself modifies his judgment when he adds that the system "today is happily undermined to its foundations."

The system is not only undermined to its foundations, but visibly crashing under the combined onslaught of political changes, the awakening of the untouchables themselves, and it must be added, the social conscience of high caste Hindus who have been startled into a rude realisation of its inhumanity. The political changes which vest power in these despised classes give to them a consciousness of strength. Also, the politics of numbers which count for so much in India, argue strongly in their favour. An addition of a few more millions to the Mahommedan religion would alter the balance of power in some of the provinces. Both the Hindus and the Mahommedans realise this important fact and much of the activity of both the communities may be motivated by the hope of the Muslims to increase their numbers on the one hand, and the fear of the Hindus that their numbers may be reduced by mass conversions. The wide-spread awakening of untouchables is also a most significant fact. Not a single day passes without some public assertion by these communities of their elementary rights. Through the length and breadth of India, in villages, towns and cities the same claims are heard: untouchables insisting on their right to worship in Hindu temples, to draw water from the same wells, to use the same public tanks, to study in the same schools. Wherever there is the least opposition on the part of the orthodox, the question becomes a public issue. The programme of the community may be summarised in one word: equality, equality in religious matters, equality in civic rights, equality in political power.

It is perhaps important to add that the awakened social consciousness of the Hindus, not only does not fight against these changes but strongly supports them. For over fifty years social reformers had pleaded for such changes. But today, the main body of Hindus are not merely sympathetic to the untouchables' claims from an intellectual point of view but are actively engaged in the fight. To a very large extent, nationalist Hindus have made the problem of untouchables their own. During the last four years Mr. Gandhi has devoted his entire energies to this question. The Harijan Sevak Sangh (Society for the service of untouchables) which is an All-India body established by him carries on unceasing propaganda for the recognition of the untouchables' rights in social and religious spheres, while also engaging itself in schemes for their economic amelioration.

There can be no question that untouchability as a feature of Hinduism will vanish within the course of the next few years. When that day comes the Hinduism that will survive will not be the same for which Manu legislated, to which the caste-society clung through centuries and which Brahmin intellectuals like Radhakrishnan try to justify today. Hindu Society such as ages have known it would have undergone a reformation, even more radical than that which Buddha attempted and more comprehensive than that which Sankara conceived.

CHAPTER IV

LEGISLATION AND RELIGIOUS NEUTRALITY

The fragmentisation of social life which is the outstanding characteristic of Hindu organisation has had one result. It has rendered impossible the growth of any principle of general obedience in Hinduism. The principle of authority on which both national and social organisation is erected has all along been absent in India. As a consequence, Hindu social life has been a wild and unregulated growth. Every kind of custom, however poisonous, found equal sanction. The practices of the Kāpālikas including human sacrifice, the customs of sati and infanticide, were as orthodox as the performance of sandhya or the worship in a temple.

In the absence of state and religious authority, social custom naturally usurped the functions of religion and arrogated to itself through pseudo-sacred writings the character of divine ordinances.

Till the East India Company, through the agitation of Rammohan Roy, took up the question of *sati* and of infanticide, there was no case of the exercise of state legislative authority for the purpose of prohibiting anti-social customs. The experience of the Mutiny however persuaded the British Government that it was safer to follow the line of least resistance and permit the Hindus to wallow in the mire of their own social customs. The policy of non-intervention in social matters continued unbroken till the Montague-Chelmsford Reform and has been only partially modified by it.

The enthronement of social customs—widely different and often conflicting—as orthodox Hinduism with religious sanction behind it was in the main the outcome of Islamic conquest. Islam is a religion in which the law is divinely revealed. The State therefore has no legislative authority. The validity of practices and customs is dependent on the fatwas of religious doctors. In the parts of India which came under Muslim sway, Hindu social life became independent of the State. The Mohammedan Kings, following the policy of the Khalifs, allowed the Hindus to be governed by their own customs and by their caste panchayats.

While the Hindu Kings at least had the obligation of regulating the growth of custom as "Kālasya Kāranam" (the originators of the age), the Mohammedan Rulers whose conception of kingly duty did not involve social legislation, could only allow custom to have unrestricted sway in communal matters. Thus though Akbar was violently opposed to the practice of *Sati* and himself intervened to save more than one unfortunate woman, the Moghul State could not prohibit this inhuman social practice. In the result Mohammedan rule in India had the extraordinary effect of encouraging an anarchic growth of social customs, each claiming to be orthodox and each asserting its sacred character. It would, however, be wrong to conclude that the co-existence of a religion with such clear cut principles and with definite authority traceable to a divinely revealed book gave birth only to disintegration and reaction. The influence of Islam on the thinking minds of India was profound, but here as in a later time, it led, in the absence of a general authority, only to the formation of sects. Individual religious leaders like Kabir and Nanak protested against the growth of irreligious customs and practices. Their influence was great and in their lifetime they started movements, as Buddha, Mahavira, Ramanuja and others before them, with the object of reforming Hindu society. But such movements resulted only in new sects and the vast and inchoate body of Hinduism continued unaffected. The lack of social authority prevented any widespread reorganisation.

There was another aspect of Muslim rule in India as affecting Hindu society to which attention may be drawn here. The Hindu States which remained independent like the Vijaynagar Empire and the Maharatta Confederacy became the champions of Hinduism on its defence. The *raison d'etre* of their existence was as the sanctuary and refuge of orthodoxy. A society on the defence is inevitably more reactionary, more anxious to preserve than to reform, to find apologists for all that had been inherited, good or bad. These States therefore considered their true function to be the conservation of the *Dharma*, the upholding of the customs and practices of the past. The duty of Kings to regulate customs and to weed out what is injurious to the body politic was obscured by the more urgent duty of warding off attacks by the enemies of the Dharma. Consequently both in the areas under direct Mohammedan rule and in the kingdoms of the Hindus society ceased to be progressive and every kind of custom came to be recognised as sacred and inviolable.

The abuse of the principle of toleration in Hinduism is itself one of the reasons for the elevation of fantastic practices to the position of religion. It is the fundamental faith of every Hindu that union with God or salvation may be attained through genuine faith in any *mārga* (path). Hinduism does not claim exclusive merit for any particular path. As Krishna says in the *Bhagvad Gita*, every path leads to God, as every river leads to the Ocean. If therefore every path leads to God, it is not open to the follower of one mārga to question the validity of another's belief. The worship of the Mariamman or the goddess of epidemics is as good a way as the most elaborate yōga; in any case no one is entitled to question another's belief. This principle of the validity of every genuine belief is the reason why Hinduism tolerates the most absurd creeds : religious sects in which the supreme worship is through human sacrifices and creeds which elevate obscene ceremonies to the position of mystic sacraments are tolerated with an indifference to social sense which may be "spiritual" but is certainly against the principles of morality. The fact is that the Hindus owing to the absence of social authority never defined the *limits of toleration.* It is no justification to argue that toleration of belief is merely a recognition of human fallibility and therefore any interference with it may lead to the suppression of truth. Toleration of belief is undoubtedly necessary. It may be my belief that human sacrifice alone can give me salvation. It may also be conceded that no one—neither State nor society—has the right of interfering with me in that belief. But the translation of that belief into practice is another matter. The question involved in that case is not one of religious toleration, but of social defence. The whole organisation of social life is based on a clear definition of the limits of toleration. A toleration which is unlimited is license and anarchy and no society could be organised on that basis. The abuse of the principle of toleration by the Hindus, the perpetuation of the most pernicious customs under the plea of religious catholicism,—a fact on which they ignorantly pride themselves—has led to the social anarchy which we call Hinduism.

From what has been said above it would be

clear that the institutions of Hinduism are the results of certain historical factors and that they are in no way concerned with religion. They are upheld by law and not by religion; they are the outcome of the acceptance of law or of custom which has the validity of law. The caste organisation, the joint family, the rights of inheritance, and the relationships arising from them are all legal and not religious. They are man-made institutions upheld by man-made law. It has been well said, that the legislation of today is to meet the social needs of yesterday: that law as a conservative force must always lag behind social necessities. When the great legal codes were evolved, there might have been social necessities which justified them. But by the time they were formulated they had by their very nature become partly antiquated. In fact when the Manava Dharma Sastra was codified many portions of it must already have been unenforceable. The evolution of the commentaries shows that many of the injunctions of the codes were modified through interpretation. The immutability of the law was not a principle with the great legislators or their commentators. The differences in interpretations and the gradual change of legal conceptions from the time of Manu to Medhadhiti—not to speak of later commentators—would clearly show that the Hindu theorists never accepted an unchangeable code of laws. If the laws are changeable then clearly the institutions which are based on such laws are equally changeable. The great weakness of Hindu society is not that the laws have not undergone change but that the changes introduced have been spasmodic, local and dependent to a large extent on the ingenuity of individual commentators. They were not in any sense a continuous renovation of legal principles, not a legislative approximation to changing social conditions. The reason for this lack of direction of social ideals and codification of laws preventing the growth of unauthorised customs of an anti-social character was undoubtedly the loss of political power. Not only was India as a whole never under a single sovereign authority, but even the political unity of Northern India which existed with occasional breaks from the time of the Mauryas (320 B.C.) to that of Harsha (637 B.C.) was broken up by the political conditions of the 8th century and irretrievably lost by the Mussalman invasions of the later ages. In the result, Hindu society continued to be governed by laws which were codified over 1,500 years ago and which were out of date even when they were codified.

The creation of an authority which could legislate on a rational basis for the Hindu community is therefore the first essential condition for the reorganisation of Hinduism. A principle of social obedience must first be established before the Hindus could be converted into a community. The underlying idea of *sanghatan* (integration) of which the Hindu leaders speak—which however few of them understand—is this doctrine of obedience. The *sanghatan* movement is a very significant one. Literally, the word sanghatan means welding together. The movement itself was started by Swami Shradhanand, the Arya Samajist leader, whose experience of the unity of Islam convinced him of the fact that the essential weakness of Hinduism lay in the fragmentisation of social life, making the very idea of a "community" alien to Hindu conception. Community involves common ideals and interests. The caste and the joint family render any idea of community impossible in Hinduism. The Sikhs, the Arya Samaj and the Radhaswamis alone of all the divisions of Hinduism have the conception of community. The *sanghatan* movement was a deliberate attempt to create the feeling of common-mindedness in Hinduism. The movement failed because no welding together was possible in Hinduism as a whole so long as there was no principle of authority and consequently no principle of obedience. The Arya Samaj has both, as the control of the community is organised through representative institutions; the Radhaswamis have a pontiff. Hinduism as a whole, containing as it does a vast variety of sects, can have no such religious authority. The necessary principle must therefore come from the secular State. Only through legislation can *sanghatan* in Hinduism be realised. The popular movement, in spite of the great impetus it had, failed as there was no machinery devised—in fact it could not be devised without creating a parallel State in India—for exacting obedience. The real beginnings of *Sanghatan* are therefore to be seen in the social legislation of the last 15 years, under the Montagu-Chelmsford Reforms—in the Hindu Religious Endowment Act of Madras, in the Civil Marriage Act and the Sarda Act of the Central Legislature. The Montagu-Chelmsford Reforms gave to India the first instalment of the Legislating State. True that the British Government in India has to its credit a formidable achievement in legislation. But generally speaking, the British Government was interested only in laws relating to administration. After the first experiments in reform by the abolition of *Sati*, infanticide and other inhuman practices, the British authorities came to the conclusion that social legislation was too dangerous an experiment for an alien Government to undertake. Consequently from the establishment of the Indian Legislative Councils in 1861 to the Montagu-Chelmsford Reforms in 1921, the record of Government is singularly barren in the field of social legislation. The few cases of legislation like the Age of Consent Act and the Anand Marriage Act, were the outcome of popular pressure and not of any desire on the part of the Government to eradicate evils in Hindu society. The Montagu-Chelmsford Act gave to the Provinces, in a limited degree, the right of legislation in social matters. In the Central Legislature also legislation on these questions became possible. For the first time, at least during the last 1,500 years, there was established a legislative authority both competent to change the laws of Hindu society and to enforce obedience to such laws through the length and breadth of India. The Civil Marriage Act and the Child Marriage Act, two of the most notable pieces of legislation enacted by the Central Legis lature, will be seen to be revolutionary from the point of view of Hindu social anarchy. The Civil Marriage Act validates marriages between men and women of different castes of Hinduism. It strikes at the root of the orthodox Brahminical conception of caste and annuls the laws of Manu and other Smriti writers. "The immutable law" prohibiting *varna sankara* or the mixture of castes ceases to operate through the length and breadth of British India. The Child Marriage Act is equally revolutionary. It has been the custom—which had almost acquired a religious sanction—for the orthodox to marry girls before the age of puberty. There was not only long tradition behind it, but it was considered compulsory in the light of certain *smritis*. The Indian legislature made this custom which had so much religious authority behind it illegal. The heavens have not fallen. Nor has Hindu religion suffered as a result. The legislating State, it is clear, cannot tolerate the social anarchy of Hinduism.

The true *Sanghatan* of Hinduism will come therefore only from the legislative activity of the State, for that alone provides the essential principle of obedience. It may well be asked why it is presumed that the State would embark on a comprehensive reorganisation of society through legislation. The answer is twofold. The democratic machinery of the provincial governments and to a certain extent of the Centre has placed power in the hands of people who find their social and political weakness in the customs, practices and laws of Hinduism. The untouchables in asking for social equality—a claim which the legislatures cannot resist—are, as we have seen, asking for the abolition of caste and society based on inequality. The women's movement, whose growing strength is one of the most significant things in India today, claims a comprehensive reform of Hindu law. We shall attempt to show that the acceptance of the programme of the women's movement would involve not only the discarding of the ancient Hindu codes, but a reconstitution of the institutions of Hinduism. Again it should not be forgotten that there is a long tradition in modern India of social reform activity which though powerless up till now, has permeated the educated classes in whom the leadership remains today.

The second reason is the character of the modern State. Professor Dicey has shown in his masterly analysis of the influence of public opinion on the law of modern England how in recent times in conservative Britain itself, the main parliamentary activity has turned towards social legislation. In other countries the process has been even more marked. The totalitarian states of Europe have as their aim the regulation of society in all its aspects. The democratic nations are not less insistent on the belief that the social life of the nation is the legitimate sphere of their activity. In Russia an all pervading socialism orders the life of the citizens. In Europe, however, as the process of legal rejuvenation of society has been continuous, the activities in this connection are not so spectacular as in the Asiatic States. 15 years of Kemalist Government have altered the face of Turkey. The revealed code of the Quran and the Shariat has been replaced by new legislation, subject to continuous modification by Parliament. Family life has been placed on a new footing by the abolition of polygamy, by the compulsory discarding of the veil, by the admission of women into all professions. There is nothing too small or too great to be considered outside the legislative activity of the Turkish Parliament. Even in the more orthodox State of Egypt, the reorientation of life which began with Jamaluddin Afgani and Mohammed Abdouh has been realised through the State. In Persia it is the same and the reforming hand of Raza Shah has not left untouched the sacred law of Islam. Though Amanullah lost his throne through his reforming zeal, Afghanistan under Nadir Shah and his successor has cautiously persisted in the path of national reorganisation. The position in China is perhaps more significant. Chiang Kai Shek has realised that his army reforms and his political power would not mean much unless Chinese society is reorganised from top to bottom. The policy of the Kuomintang has therefore been a twofold one—consolidation of the Middle Kingdom under one authority and the reorganisation of society through the *New Life Movement*. The latter seeks to replace the old social order and to give effect to a real *Sanghatan*. The above examples would prove that the modern state is based on the conception of a purposive organisation of society. It is not merely an administrative institution; essentially, it is the executive organ of the complex of social forces and exists in order to mould, direct and organise society according to the needs of the times. In States which have lagged behind in this matter, like Turkey, Persia and China, this aspect of the

State is especially emphasised. Equally in India, the State in the years to come will concern itself more with the organisation of life, in the social and economic fields—and that will be the real *sanghatan.*

That in this welding together much that we now consider the differentiating characteristics of Hindu society will disappear is certain. Institutions like caste, the segregation of classes, and the existence of untouchability are fundamentally opposed to the democratic ideals on which at least the provinces in the future will be governed. The incompatibility between caste and democracy which has already been emphasised and the strength which democracy will gain in this fight by the revolt of the suppressed classes and by the pressure of economic forces render any opposition which might arise from the vested interests of priest—craft negligible and easy to overcome.

The champions of social anarchy have already awakened to the danger that faces them. 'The varnāsrama dharma swaraj party,' which was organised under the patronage of Sankaracharyas and other religious dignitaries voiced their fear before the Joint Select Committee of Parliament. They held that the new provincial and Federal

Governments were likely to depart from the policy of "religious neutrality"—an euphemism for deliberate inactivity in social legislation—and that the structure of Hinduism would thereby be seriously endangered. The familiar cry of religion in danger was raised and the possibility of a large scale revolt like the Mutiny was hinted at. The Varnasrama Dharma Swarajya Sangh was undoubtedly correct in its appreciation of the position. A legislative State and social anarchy cannot coexist. The State-conception postulates the right of the people to change the conditions under which they live and the bewildering confusion of Hindu life has been the outcome of the absence of this State conception all through Indian history. The death-knell of that anarchy has been sounded and it has now become possible to eradicate the customs which have for so long a time stood in the way of the Hindus being organised into a community.

CHAPTER V

THE CLAIMS OF WOMEN

We have, earlier in this discussion, alluded to the importance of the women's movement to the general question of the reorganisation of Hindu life. No attempt is made here to describe the origin and growth of that movement or its activities. But it is necessary for a clear understanding of our problem to examine those parts of the programme which would inevitably lead to organic changes in Hindu society.

The Indian women's movement is not one which is confined to Hindu women though in the circumstances of India it is predominantly Hindu in membership. Its programme is also general, though much of it deals with the special disabilities that women in the different communities are subjected to. Questions like the abolition of Parda, equal chances in public services, representation on political bodies, reform of education are common to most communities. But besides these, there are also special problems of different communities with which the movement is concerned, rights of Hindu widows, sale of women in certain communities etc. Generally speaking the activities of the movement may be classified under three heads:

(1) acquisition of property rights,

(2) social legislation,

(3) equality of political rights.

The subsidiary activities relating to education, social hygiene, medical attention etc., though of importance, are incidental to the backwardness of India and do not specially relate to women. The acquisition of property rights, include the questions of the daughter's share or the relation of the female children to the joint family, the wife's property or the economic relationship between the husband and the wife and the widow's estate. Each of these questions affects the fundamental conception of Hindu social organisation. It is however worthy of note that the answer of Hindu law to these questions is not uniform and that under certain schools the position of women in regard to property is more liberal than under others.

But minor differences apart, the basic doctrine is that women have no right of independent inheritance and even where a widow is entitled to her *Stridhan* (dowry) she has only a life interest in it. The claim of the women in each of these three categories relating to property strikes at the root of the Hindu Joint family. The daughter's claim to inheritance, if accepted, would revolutionise the conception of the family. The Hindu family from the earliest times never considered a girl child as belonging to it. In the words of Kalidasa a daughter is like an ornament in pawn which has to be surrendered to the rightful owner when he claims it. Yaksha's Nirukta (II, 4 Anandāsrama Edition, p. 208) declares "They give away to others the female children. There exist dāna, vikraya, and atisarga of female but not of a male. . . ." Dāna means gift, vikraya means sale, atisarga means abandonment (to which in later times may be added infanticide). It is true that Durgacharya the commentator tries to explain these three methods of disposal of daughters by saying that dāna (gift) means giving away in marriage, vikraya (sale) means acceptance of payment for marriage and atisarga (abandonment) means freedom to choose. The persistence of the tradition of the female child being unwelcome in the Hindu family—witness the existence of female infanticide even today in certain communities, like the *Dogras* of Jammu, would show that Yaksha's three methods of disposal of daughters deals with the customs of the Hindu society of his time by which unwanted daughters were got rid of. The Hindu daughter is in fact not a member of the family. The claim of the daughter to inherit her share in the family to which she is born is essentially a denial of the Hindu position and an assertion of the right to be treated on equality with sons. The problem in earlier times was not serious when every girl was presumed to marry and join some other family group. But today it takes a different aspect. Modern society which does not permit such short cuts as female infanticide, or even *atisarga* (abandonment) is increasingly faced with the problem of unmarried women. The raising of the age of marriage by legislation will increase the urgency of this problem. Economic freedom which women justly claim will add to the growing demand of the daughters for their legitimate share in the family property. In any case the unmarried women introduce into the joint family an element altogether alien to Hindu conception and the recognition of their claims, which the legislature would not be able to resist would be a major breach in the citadel of Hindu orthodoxy.

The problem of wife's property is equally complicated. If women are entitled to separate estates, acquired either through *Stridhan* (dowry) or by individual acquisition, the unity of the family is bound to disappear. It cannot be too strongly emphasised that the complete economic dependence of women is a necessary postulate of the indissoluble marriage under the patriarchal system. The acquisition of private property by women and their right to maintenance in case of separation means nothing short of the formulation in time of a new code of marriage and family laws. The claim of the widow to an independent share in the estate of her husband will also be seen to be based on a doctrine which undermines the Hindu social organisation. A financially independent widow, permitted by law to marry, involves a change in the permanence of family ties which is the basic conception of Hindu social life.

It is clear from the above discussion that the claim of women to inherit property, when accepted, would involve a revolution, unseen but fundamental, in Hindu life. Resistance to these claims has become impracticable. In fact orthodoxy has already yielded in advance and there is no serious opposition to these claims. New conditions have created new problems. The unmarried daughter, the economically independent wife, the educated widow—these are problems which the sociologists of ancient Hindu life did not have to deal with. Hindu laws do not take into consideration the problems created by their existence. In the result any solution of these urgent social problems must involve a radical change in Hindu Law. The personal law of the Hindus, so long safeguarded by orthodoxy and maintained even under Mohammadan and Christian rule, has visibly broken down in the face of women's economic claims.

The social legislation for which the women's movement agitates is equally hostile to orthodox Hindu theory. The main claims in this connection are the abolition of polygamy, the right of civil marriage, the raising of the Age of Consent for marriage and the right of divorce. The abolition of polygamy and the raising of the age of consent, reforms which are not likely to meet with strenuous opposition, will both increase the number of unmarried women, modifying thereby the economic structure of the Hindu family. The right of civil marriage within the Hindu community is already secured under British Indian Legislation. The enlargement of its scope and the removal of economic restrictions under which civil marriage is now permitted, must modify even the theory of caste. The right of divorce would again involve a fundamental change in the law of Hinduism. No doubt, orthodoxy will fight to the last ditch on this question but it is well to remember that in certain orthodox Hindu States like Baroda, the principle of divorce is recognised and permitted under law.

The claim for political equality has in the main been conceded. There are women representatives in all the provincial legislatures. They sit along with men in district boards, municipalities, and other institutions of public life. The Working Committee of the National Congress has for many years had at least one woman on it. In most of the provincial ministries women are represented, while in the United Provinces, Mrs. Vijaya Luxmi Pandit holds an important portfolio.

The importance of this change is in connection with the legislative enforcement of the women's claims. Women's vote is an important factor in the elections to the legislatures. The presence of elected women representatives in the legislatures secured under the Act of 1935 would make their influence constantly felt. Social legislation must therefore figure prominently in the programme of all parties and the conflict between the legislating State and the social anarchy of Hinduism will be carried to a decisive stage by the women's movement.

The importance of the subsidiary activities of the women's movement should not also be forgotten. Especially the problem of women's education has an influence on these questions which cannot be exaggerated. If the Hindus desired to safeguard their worn out institutions they should have kept their women in ignorance emphasising to them as immutable law the doctrine of *Pati-devata* or "the husband-god." Though the orthodox did not fail to observe the disastrous results that would follow the education of women and consequently denied it to their own children, they were unable to prevent others from educating their girls. Today there is a premium on educated women even from the point of view of marriage. The orthodox themselves are unable to resist the demand. Naturally educated women cannot be forced to believe in the ideal of *pati-devata* and to be content with the faith that worship of the husband—however degraded, immoral and unmanly he be—is equal to worship of God himself. The ancient Indian ideals of womanhood come in for examination and criticism in the light of reason and common sense. They see that each individual personality whether of man or of woman has value in itself and the compulsory merging of women's individuality in man's has no justification either in reason or in religion. The Hindu religion has never taught the inferiority of woman. On the other hand, the equality of women is emphasised in all Hindu sects. It is the law of the Hindus and not their religion which denies women property rights, compels children to marry and enforces the prohibition of the remarriage of widows. Further, education and intellectual discontent are inseparable. The awakening of thought in women as a result of education involves an examination by them of the basis of the social customs and laws under which they live.

The women's movement in emphasising education is really sharpening the axe with which to clear away the wild growths of Hindu social life. Education involves new moral and ethical conceptions, and an unchanging moral code laid down thousands of years ago or based on the growth of local customs cannot satisfy an educated mind.

It may be argued that the rigid code of the Catholic Church has not been weakened with the education of women and it is not necessary that education should break down the social code of Hinduism. That argument is based on fallacious reasoning. The social code of the Catholics, so far as it is governed by the Church, is not an immutable code. The Church through the Papacy and the *Curia* provides a machinery for constant reinterpretation to suit the changing moral opinion of the world. The absence of social authority in Hinduism makes such gradual modification impossible.

The re-examination of the principles of social life by Hindu women is therefore one of the most important features of Indian life today. It arises from the awakening of their own minds to changed social needs; from their discontent with an utterly unsatisfying ideal which taking refuge behind religion, denies them essential rights for a free and independent life: from their ambition, arising from education to participate in the life of the nation and to shape its future. To some extent its inspiration comes from the West. The position of women in the life of European nations has undoubtedly helped in the awakening. Educated women cannot be made to shut their eyes to the important part that women play in the intellectual and social life of Europe. But apart from this influence and the modernism of thought which it has infused, their own needs have given the most irresistible impetus to this movement. The evidence for the genuinely independent character of the women's movement—a fact which makes its claims imperative and unanswerable—is the nation wide response to its appeal. From Cape Comorin to Kashmir, from Assam to the North-West Frontier, the women's voice is now being heard. Twelve years ago a women's movement as such did not exist. The problems arising in that sphere were considered to be special concern of Social Reformers. But when the first Women's Conference met 12 years ago it became with startling rapidity an All-India movement. It viewed Indian life as a whole, attacked problems in the spirit of practical needs and gathered such strength as to become a definitely national movement. Its wide appeal is a standing challenge to Hindu orthodoxy. No more can proposals of social reform be shelved on the ground that the Hindu society will rise up in opposition. It is the most conservative section of the people—the women—who demand the reforms and provide the driving force for social legislation. The Hindu social anarchy has never faced such a challenge and can never survive such an attack.

The significant fact which needs to be emphasised in this connection is that though the programme of the women's movement is radical in the sense that it involves fundamental changes in the law of the community and a consequent reorganisation of the social institutions, its leadership is not with what may be called the radical elements in Hindu society. The Maharanis of the most orthodox Hindu States like Baroda and Travancore, Brahmin women of the highest social standing, wives and daughters of high officers, are all equally associated in the direction of its policy. The women's movement can therefore be said to represent fully the mind of the educated women of India; and its minimum policy which we have discussed above cannot be resisted by any party.

What is the cumulative effect of the women's demands on Hindu life. Briefly stated it is nothing less than the entire reorganisation of Hindu society on a modern basis. While the demand is in regard to all communities, its effect on each is different. On Hinduism it has the most far-reaching effect. The acceptance of the least important of the claims of women would effect the so-called immutable laws of Hinduism and change its social structure. The gradual enforcement of its whole programme would create a revolution in Hindu society—establishing for it a modern code of laws, a new morality, a new principle of social relationship. The system of caste and of joint family would disappear : the institutes of the ancient law-givers would give place to more rational codes : customs and practices which exist on the pretended sanction of religion but which are merely the results of social reaction would cease to be observed. The survival of the Hindus may therefore be legitimately said to be dependent on the success of the women's movement.

CHAPTER VI

MAYA AND "THE IDEALIST VIEW"

Unconnected with religion and unrelated to social institutions there are certain ideas, practices and customs which stand in the way of Hindu regeneration. They may be discussed under two main groups: (1) ideas and customs which enervate the race and (2) ideas and customs which cause social degeneration. In the first category fall such ideas of the futility of this world, pacificism, vegetarianism and the general pessimism of Hindu life. In the second the prohibition of inter-marriage, the *mlecha* (barbarian) attitude towards others and the lack of national feeling. The creation of a new outlook towards life and the eradication of the feeling of passivity resulting from centuries of subjection must form the essential feature of any comprehensive scheme of Hindu regeneration.

The idea of the futility of this world which is probably the most widely prevalent conception among the Hindus is at the root of much of the weakness of Hindu life. In essence it is a pseudo-religious conception being merely the popular perversion of the profound doctrine of Māya. The doctrine of Māya is the philosophical view which declares that God alone is real and that all other is illusion. No doubt from that point of view all expect the Ultimate is unreal and illusory. But this conception provides no justification for the common belief in the futility of human action. The reconciliation between the belief in the sole reality of God and the necessity of action in this world is provided in all the sublimity of the highest spiritual revelation in the most sacred of all Hindu scriptures, the Gita itself. From the religious point of view therefore there can be no justification for the common Hindu attitude of passivity on the ground that the world itself is unreal. That such is the common outlook no one could deny. The combination of the Māyā vāda with the popular view of the doctrine of Karma has produced in the Hindu mind the attitude of despair, helplessness and pessimism. All the misfortunes of this world are traced to this false interpretation of Karma and inactivity in fighting fate is justified by an appeal to the illusoriness of the world. Analysed, this attitude is no more than a philosophical justification of *defaitism*. Centuries of political subjection and worldly misfortune had to be reconciled with racial pride. No activity of any kind seemed to be able to retrieve the lost fortunes of the Hindu community; and the philosophic doctrines of Māya and Karma seemed to provide a ready made explanation and justification for the misfortunes of this life. The doctrine of Karma was perverted to find the explanation: the doctrine of Māya was appealed to in justification of its passive acceptance. The pernicious effects of misinterpretation of these doctrines and their almost universal acceptance cannot be too strongly emphasised. An attitude of helplessness against destiny dominates all aspects of life. If children die through lack of medical attention, if insanitary conditions create epidemics, if fields show a diminishing return through uneconomic cultivation—there is Karma to explain it: and the illusoriness of the world to prevent human effort. In fact as a result of this philosophy of *defaitism*, national initiative has been totally extinguished.

"An idealist view of life" about which one hears so much in academic circles may be valuable. Indeed it may provide a just balancing between the spiritual and material aspects of life. But in a community so dominated by the spirit of helplessness and from which all initiative has vanished it is the pragmatist view of life that is important. To preach "idealism", when the practical attitude necessary even for existence is lacking is but to provide another excuse for the passivity of the Hindu mind. It should not be understood that the present writer denies the validity of the idealist view. What is emphasised is the necessity equally of a practical view of life, or the importance of the realisation of ideas through institutions, and of the balancing of material and ideal considerations. Where one aspect of life is exaggerated as in India, the immediate necessity is to restore the balance by emphasising the other. In the conditions of Hindu life today to preach a philosophy based on the importance of spirit is to forget what India lacks. Philosophy may be the discovery of the ultimate truth: but ultimate truth being so difficult to discover and when discovered so difficult to apply to the practical necessities of life, it has a habit of degenerating into scholastic speculation. And woe is the result of that society which finds comfort for its misery in the verbosity and hair splitting of self-styled philosophers.

The re-assertion of a practical outlook and the exorcism of the paralysing spirit of false philosophies are therefore essential if Hindus desire to live and not merely to exist as they do today. That is where Mahatma Gandhi touches the fundamental truth. The dynamic character of Gandhiji's teaching, in spite of many things that appear crude and of the dependence on inner voice, lies in the emphasis on practical life : activity directed towards the better organisation of society, the greater material comfort of the poor and the depressed, the establishment of equality as the basis of national life. Others may quarrel with the philosophical basis of Gandhiji's thought but what he stands for is essentially a principle of activism, a practical attitude towards social problems and a faith in human initiative and reason. A man of the spirit, he is equally a materialist in the belief that conditions of life must improve for a society to advance. Gandhiji's contribution to national life is that he has through his own example and by his teaching shaken off the stupor of despair and of submission to fate in which Hindus lived.

The pacificism of the Hindus is equally a reflection of their helplessness. Undoubtedly *ahimsa* (non-injury) is the highest good and no one denies that man should strive for the highest good. But human society can only be based on compromise and the reply of the Buddha himself to a sceptic who questioned him on the injury caused by speaking truth may be quoted here:

"Speech that Tathagata knows to be untrue, false and useless and also unpleasant and disagreeable to others, he does not speak.

That which he knows to be true, real, but useless and also unpleasant and disagreeable to others he does not speak.

That which he knows to be true, real and useful and also unpleasant and disagreeable to others, in that case he knows the right time to express it.

Speech that he knows to be untrue, false and useless and also pleasant and agreeable to others, he does not speak:

That which is true, real, but useless and also pleasant and agreeable to others, that too he does not speak:

But that which is true, real and useful and also pleasant and agreeable to others, in that case he knows the right time to express it."

The practice of *ahimsa* therefore *has the limitation of the greater good.* A thief cannot be allowed to escape on the ground that to catch him will be to injure him, because non-injury to the society is the greater good which may not be forgotten. And after all, what more convincing argument against an enervating pacificism is necessary than the doctrines of *Gita.* And yet, the false doctrine has so permeated the vast mass of Hindus that in spite of the Kshatriya being an honoured caste, the profession of the soldier is looked down upon by the masses. "Philosophy" has much to answer for in India.

It is a matter of satisfaction that Hindu leaders are now awakening to the necessity of fighting this enervating cult of pacificism. It is significant that so orthodox a Brahmin as the late Bal Gangadhar Tilak should have emphasised the importance of national defence to the Hindus and should have found inspiration for it in the Gita. Equally significant it is that leaders of Hindu Mahasabha should have taken upon themselves the duty of arousing the martial spirit in the community by the establishment of military schools.

The food question is another important aspect of the Hindu problem. The Hindu is prevented by his religious customs from eating various kinds of food. What authority there is in religion for these prohibitions, it is difficult to know, when the Kashmiri Brahmins can eat meat, the Bengalis fish, the Kshatriyas all kinds of non-vegetarian food except beef and yet remain *orthodox*.*

In any case food is presumably a matter for medical science and not for religion. And yet Hindus would deny medicine its sphere and allow religious customs to dictate what they should eat.

*There is a general belief that Hinduism prohibits the eating of flesh. Strange as it may seem all authoritative texts on the other hand preach the value of meat food. The Ramayana says:

"Servants quickly served flesh meat variously dressed fot the use of Rama". In the Mahabharata it is stated:

"Cooks....served them large pieces of meat roasted on spits and meat cooked as curries.....Young buffaloes roasted on spits and dressed by dropping *ghee* thereon; the same fried in *ghee*....large haunches of venison boiled in different ways."

In Uttara Rama Charita of Bhavabhuti, one Brahmin boy explains the disappearance of a calf by stating that it had been killed and cooked for the benefit of the visiting sage and adds:

"Why know you not, the vedas which enshrine our holy law direct the householder shall offer those who in the law are skilled, the honied meal and with it the *flesh of ox* or *calf* or *goat*!"

One of the most important things done in India in recent times was the experiment conducted under government auspices on the nutritive value of the food eaten in different parts of India. What that experiment proved is that the food eaten by the Hindus in what may be described as the orthodox areas of Hinduism, Bengal and Madras had not sufficient nutritive value. No wonder that Dr. Moonje the champion of militant Hinduism is never tired of emphasising the necessity of a scientific rearrangement of Hindu dietary as a preliminary to all reform.

Connected with this question is the restriction on what, for want of a better name, is called inter-dining. Hindu social custom does not permit members of one sub-caste to partake food with members of other sub-castes. An orthodox Brahmin from Malabar cannot share a meal with a Brahmin of Kashmir though the claim of both is equal in Brahminhood. In fact orthodoxy is judged sometimes solely on the ground whether you eat your food with any one outside your own special sub-caste. One who does not eat with any one except the members of his own family is respected as the most orthodox; one who is lax to the extent of having food with others of the same caste, (though not the same sub-caste) is considered less orthodox while those who overlook the restrictions are altogether heterodox whose conduct deserves the greatest censure. The importance of this restriction from the point of view of the unity of the community need not be emphasised. The Hindu sub-castes, not permitted to inter-marry or to "inter-dine" remain isolated units almost alien to each other.

It is unnecessary to examine other customs. The fundamental fact to be remembered is the supremacy of customs in Hindu life. It is custom that is King in Hinduism. It has been well said that what differentiates a civilised society from an uncivilised one is its attitude towards customs. In civilised societies custom itself is not entitled to general acceptance unless it has a clear social purpose that justifies it. In primitive societies the validity of custom does not depend on the social purpose it claims to serve, but on the fact that "it has been so from time immemorial." The mere fact that such has been the practice in the past is supposed to be sufficient justification for its continuance.

In civilised society, even the most ancient custom has to prove itself in every generation.

Its authority is challenged continually and its claim to usefulness is tested. The Hindus unfortunately have so long been prone to accept their customs as the accumulated wisdom of their ancestors, even when a casual examination would have shown that the growth of most of their customs has been haphazard, unconscious and without any useful social purpose. It is the fact of the society being in a perpetual state of defence that led them to attach an exaggerated importance to every custom which came down to them. The most important function of Hindu thought today is to re-examine all customs and traditions and to scrutinise from the point of view of social usefulness each one of the *tabus* insisted upon in the name of religion.

CHAPTER VII

CAN THE HINDUS SURVIVE?

The argument in the preceding pages has been directed to show that the survival of the Hindu peoples as an effective body in the world depends on their transformation into a *community*. The elementary fact that stares even the casual observer in the face is that Hindu theory does not provide for the conception of a community. The communal conceptions it evolved were the elementary ones of family and sub-caste. Ideologically it created a caste-society which was merely a principle of social division and not of social integration. The incompatibility of the caste idea and the community idea has been emphasised. Community means integration on the basis of common ideals. It means control and direction and necessarily involves a highly developed principle of social obedience. Caste is based on the opposite principle, the principle of division. Any tendency towards social integration must therefore inevitably break down caste.

It should be mentioned that the thinking sections of the Hindus have begun to realise that their survival as a people depends on social integration. By contrast with other communities like the Christians and the Muslims, the Hindus have begun to feel and act as a community. Once again as a matter of defence, a Hindu feeling has come into existence and the organisation of the community on the basis of that feeling is the main problem which faces not only the Hindus but India as a whole.

There is an important difference between the Hindu feeling which has come into existence during the last quarter of a century and similar tendencies in earlier times. There was undoubtedly a genuine Hindu feeling created at the time of the Mohammedan conquest. But that feeling was religious and not secular. Mr. Ketkar has pointed out in his History of Caste that the overthrow of the Hindu Princes by the Muslim invaders led to a great increase in the prestige of the Brahmins. The secular Kshatriya power was broken but as the Hindus in their social affairs continued to be independent, the Mohammedan conquest only strengthened the hold of the Brahmins. The

Hindu feeling of the time was responsible therefore for the most extreme religious reaction. Caste became more rigid; social customs without the directing hand of the secular state, usurped the authority of religion. No feeling of the community developed as the Hindu people got more and more disintegrated.

It must, however, be conceded that the dominance of the Brahmins at this time saved the Hindus from dissolution. While the Kshatriyas and other upholders of secular authority compromised with Islam for the sake of political power—thereby yielding social leadership exclusively to the Brahmins—the priestly classes protected what they considered to be the Dharma to the best of their ability. Under their influence Hinduism withdrew more and more into its shell and all its anti-social characteristics became exaggerated. But it is well to remember that but for Brahmin leadership at the time, there would have been no Hinduism left today for others to reform or to regenerate.

The main difference between the Hindu feeling today and of the earlier times is therefore the secular character of the present day movement. The leaders of the Hindu Mahasabha, no less than the social reformers, recognise that what is required if Hinduism is to survive as an effective force, is to create the unity of feeling among the different sections of Hindu peoples which alone can transform a population into a community. Hence the Sanghatan movement. Hence the Harijan Sevak Sangh; hence again the legislative proposals of social reformers (both Princes and public men) meant to break down the barriers between the social groups of Hinduism. The Hindu religion is left well alone. Religious dogmas and doctrines cannot be reformed: but secular society can and must be reformed if it is to live. This essential truth has been brought home to the Hindus of the present generation.

It may be and has been argued that social reform is as old as Hinduism itself and that in spite of the greatness of the leaders of reform movements from the Buddha to Mahatma Gandhi, Hinduism has remained unaffected. True indeed, but again the circumstances today are so different that much lesser men than Buddha, Nanak, Ramanuja and Gandhi may be able to do what they failed to achieve.

Where the problem in India today differs from the problem as it has existed during the last 2,000 years is not that there is widespread protest against social abuses but that the motive force of the protest is different. At every age since the time of the Buddha, there have been vigorous movements of reform in Indian Society. In fact India's claim to civilisation is not based so much on her social institutions as in her movements of protest. From Gautama Buddha to Mohandas Gandhi it is an imposing array of men that India can claim to have produced to combat the evils of her social institutions. But these great men though they gave expression to the protests of national conscience did not have the machinery of the organised State to give effect to their reforms. The principle of social obedience in India remained familial and local and Hinduism continued to live much in the same way as in pre-historic times in spite of her great men. The difference today is that such a machinery has been created with the help of Indians themselves and is available for the radical reform of Hindu Society.

Then again there is the distribution of political power. The political unity that has been created in India has now found a legislative basis on an electorate which may not be democratic enough but is all the same distributed over the different grades of society. It is neither the Brahmins nor the Kshatriyas alone who exercise the power in the new State. On the other hand the classes which have so far been excluded by Hindu society from exercising any influence in social organisation have been expressly given such power. The women, the untouchables, the vast masses who so far had neither part nor lot in the ordering of social life have been invested with power to decide for themselves the conditions under which they live. If the creation of the All India State is an undoubted danger to the self-governing character of Hindu social institutions, the introduction of democracy by investing the masses with political power is to provide the dynamite for the destruction of social institutions based on hereditary inequality. Democracy may not be an ideal system of government. It may indeed have more weaknesses than an aristocracy of intellect or even of birth which is conscious of its high social purpose. But there is one fundamental characteristic of democracy which is of the utmost importance to our problem. It involves the ordering of society consciously and purposefully by the people themselves and not either by unregulated customs, by a revealed code or by "the remote speculations of isolated thinkers." It is true that democracy is not inherently dynamic. The forward impulse must undoubtedly come from outside for democracy to work towards an active realisation of social ideals. The great and undoubted discontent with the conditions of life which has moved the vast mass of untouchables, the insistent claims of women for the recognition of their position, the ethical urge of the social reformers and the political need of the Hindus themselves in competition with other communities, will provide the necessary irresistible motive force. The arousing of energies in all classes of Hindus has been the first fruit of democratic institutions in India. The non-Brahmin movement in Madras, the threat of the untouchables to leave the Hindu fold if their social claims are not recognised, the attack on Hindu personal law by the women have been the direct result of the distribution of political power to the masses. The frozen immobility of Hindu society, ice bound by the thick layer of custom, is melting under the warm flow of democratic authority.

Another and equally important difference between the challenge to Hinduism today and on all previous occasions is the revolutionary change in the material setting of life in India. In olden times distances rendered all-India repercussion to ideas almost impossible. Reforms and changes tended therefore to be local. With the development of railways, air communication, posts and telegraphs, the factor of distance has been practically annihilated. The range of Buddha's activities was confined to Magadha: that of Gandhi's extends over the whole of India. Sankara had to go walking from place to place and then could reach only the elite. Today the message of change is published through thousands of papers and reaches the commonest man. The radio and the cinema have already come into the field of popular education and their influence in creating a consciousness of unity will increase day by day. A further and growing factor is the industrialisation of the towns. The vast concentration of people in the centres of industry creates problems of social organisation which the Hindus never contemplated. The silent operation of these changes in the circumstances of daily life is fast creating a revolution which neither caste nor custom can arrest or limit.

The explosive character of modern technique, machinery, transport, living equipment etc. is also not sufficiently appreciated in India today. Undoubtedly these altered conditions have had only a limited influence up till now owing to the fact that they were confined to urban areas. But the position is being rapidly changed. The emphasis of all national activity has shifted to the villages. The Government and the National Congress vie with each other in their schemes for village uplift. The Congress even holds its annual sessions in villages instead of in capital cities in order to take the message of political freedom to the masses. The programme of rural reconstruction to which the Government, the Congress and the States are equally committed involves a complete change in the material conditions of village life.

Another factor which is becoming increasingly important is the appeal of socialism. The socialist party is a growing influence among the peasants and workers of India. It challenges directly every social institution to which Hindus have attached importance. The socialist creed not only implies but directly postulates a revolution in Hindu social life. It has come as a message of hope to the oppressed peasants, to the downtrodden untouchables and to the workers of the towns. It is no argument against the influence of socialist ideas to say that in a medieval society like India, a socialist state could not immediately come into existence. What is important for our purpose is the fact that the spread of socialist theories has further undermined Hindu social organisations among the peasants and workers in the villages which had so long been out of the range of the reformer's activities.

The conditions that limited the success of all previous efforts to reorganise the Hindu people have all disappeared. More, new conditions have come into existence which not only ensure success, but make the changes inevitable. The question whether the Hindus will survive which might easily have been doubted in the 19th century is no longer difficult to answer. Not only will the Hindus survive, but they will under proper leadership become effective as a community in the affairs of the world.

What indeed is the problem which faces them. It is the integration of the Hindu peoples into a community with purposive direction of social forces and energies and fulfilling the ethical and moral conceptions of its members. For centuries now, it has been in the grip of the long agony of a wasting disease because the energies of the whole body could not be concentrated on any common purpose. To resist its ravages it is not sufficient that palliatives should be applied. The body itself should be made stronger, healthier and more vigorous. That rejuvenation, it is now recognised, can be successful only if all parts of the body-social are united into a single whole. The weakening of thought, the absence of enterprise and initiative, the decline of vigour—in fact all the symptoms of general debility will disappear only if the society becomes organised to receive ideas—which are its food—and to transform those ideas into practice.

The choice has fortunately been made. It has been made when the decision was taken by the British Government to transfer political power. To a large extent the choice was made by the Hindus themselves. It is their agitation for freedom that has been responsible for the creation of the new conditions. No doubt few of those who clamoured loudly for the freedom of India realised that in asking for this change they were undermining the social structure of Hinduism which they held dear. It would have been a matter for disquieting reflection to most of the leaders of the Congress in the earlier generation if they witnessed the logical outcome of their demand for freedom in the Resolutions of the Women's Conference and in the radical declarations of untouchable leaders. But the safety of Hinduism and the greatness of India lie undoubtedly in the fact that the claim for political power has unloosened the pent up discontent of the socially oppressed and has enabled the movement for the reorganisation of Hinduism to assume a secular character, without affecting its religious life.

The governing fact of the twentieth century in India has been the political organisation of the Hindus on a national basis as exemplified by the Indian National Congress. Even the champions of orthodoxy were misled (from their point of view) into this activity by a vague feeling of nationalism, little realising that the claim of political emancipation involved by necessary inference the breakdown of orthodoxy itself. Political activity is based on two essential implications, each dangerous to orthodoxy and when combined utterly destructive of its very foundations: firstly political activity, based as it is on the desire for national power, implies that life in this world is of immediate concern. The domain of orthodoxy has always lain in the conception that life in the other world alone mattered. Organised political activity changed this idea by emphasising the importance of freedom in this world. It gave a new ideal to the people, the ideal of economic prosperity and material comfort which would follow political emancipation; presented a new view of history, by which the miseries in which the masses lived were traced not *to karma* but to a system of government: and exposed the weakness of Hindu social system in the necessary reorganisation to gain this political power. All these factors, it need hardly be said, were dangerous to the dominion of orthodoxy.

Secondly, organised political activity postulated the principle that society was subject to human ordering. Otherwise there could be no justification for the claim to political power. The dynamic character of this theory in its relation to social life began to be clear only with the development of such agitations as that of the untouchables. But it should be noted that it was always inherent in the political movement itself. In order that the political movement might be irresistible it had to get the support of the masses. The appeal to the masses could only bring out the patent fact that political emancipation can never be complete without social emancipation. Orthodoxy had through political organisation dug its own grave.

Other causes which have helped to establish

Hindu social thought on a secular basis may also be alluded to. The penetration of education, though by no means deep, has it must be remembered, not been confined to the higher ranks of social hierarchy. Even the untouchables came under the influence of modern education, the chief characteristic of which has been a denial of authority. The advanced theories of modern social science became available to all who could read and understand without restrictions of caste or creed. No social theory based on the vague authority of age long custom—without the sanction either of faith or of reason—could withstand this challenge. Further, the advantage that orthodoxy had in the fact that India had no history slowly vanished as the researches of scholars reconstructed the political evolution and the social growth of Hinduism. The canons of modern criticism began to be applied to the texts which had so long been blandished as authoritative. One example may be given here to show how the revival of critical scholarship has effected Hindu social structure. The inhuman custom of unapproachability in Malabar was upheld as a religious institution on the ground that it had sanction in Sankara Smriti. The name of the great Sankara was invoked and the religious, even when they disapproved of the custom, remained silent under the weight of Sankara's authority. A critical examination of the so-called Smriti however proved that the text which was held up as authority was itself a very late forgery and was entitled to no respect. The reconstruction of history was equally disastrous to the claim of permanence to Hindu social institutions. The patient researches of historians proved that many of the customs which claimed antiquity as their sanction were not prevalent in historical times. Thus for example, it was the belief till recent times that Hindu religion prohibited journey across the seas. The Brahmins enforced the punishment of social exclusion against all who dared to break this custom and the Ruling Princes of Cochin and Travancore prohibited till less than 10 years ago the entry of such people into Hindu temples. Historical research has however knocked the bottom out of this custom. The history of the Hindu colonial Empires in Java, Sumatra, Siam and Cambhoj clearly established that in the days of Hindu political independence no such restrictions existed. Further it was proved to satisfaction that orthodox Brahmins led such expeditions overseas. Other social customs too, which were considered a part of *Sanatana Dharma* (of immutable laws) such as the prohibition of widow remarriage and the early marriage of girls were found not to have been enforced in historical times. For example there is incontestable historical evidence to prove the fact that Chandra Gupta II married the widow of his brother, as Bāna himself alludes in the Kadambari. That Kshatriya women always retained their freedom to marry after growing up to maturity has never been denied; but that in the case of other castes also including orthodox Brahmins e.g., Kashmiri Pandits and Nambudiri Brahmins of Malabar, child marriage was never the custom is now being widely appreciated. The growth of the study of Indian history has thus breached the citadels of orthodoxy in places where it claimed until now undisputed sway.

Even the idea of the Golden Age has become a weapon in the hands of the antagonists. If all was well in the Golden Age, it is quite clear that the present state of society represents a fall from those ideal conditions. The conception of an unchanging and eternal social order and a Golden Age of the past are clearly irreconcilable. If society can degenerate and Golden Ages can vanish then the immutability of social laws can have no meaning. A changing social order such as the theory of the Golden Age postulates, must either predicate that the present society is not based on the immutable laws, or that such laws can only be given effect to under conditions which are ideal. The conception of the *Yugas* (or ages) in Hindu social theory as explained in the Mahabharata is also based on the idea that social direction alone can create the conditions of the Golden Age. In any case, degeneration involves a theory of social regression which invites an examination of the validity of laws and customs which have led to the change and is consequently opposed to the permanence of social structure.

Nor can the influence of other religions in the realm of social organisation be forgotten. The conversion of large bodies of untouchables to Christianity has had the effect of awakening those classes to the inequalities which Hindu social organisation enforces on them. While it is true that an untouchable by becoming a Christian does not necessarily improve his material conditions, it is undeniable that he becomes thereby a member of a world organisation which has as its fundamental conception the equality of human beings. He is armed with a new social theory. He gains a new outlook on life, which rejects all ideas emphasising his own natural inferiority. The influence of Christian conversions on the Hindu untouchables is perhaps more important than even the condition of the converts. The belief in Hindu religion may not be affected by the preaching of Christianity: but inevitably there is aroused a social consciousness which rejects emphatically "the whole code of fraud and woe" which the caste system and its concomitants mean for them. The declaration of Dr. Ambedkar, the leader of the depressed classes that though born a Hindu, he was determined not to die as one is the assertion of this spirit of revolt. The depressed classes may remain Hindus in religion but will no longer accept the immutability of caste laws which deny them human rights and compel them to live in degradation. The rival social theories of other religions have made the position untenable for Hinduism.

CHAPTER VIII

CONCLUSION

The thesis of this book, as explained at the outset, is to demonstrate that the survival of the Hindus as an effective people is possible only if from being a complex of innumerable social groups, they become a single social organism, governed by laws which approximate to their ethical conception, and which enable them constantly to renovate themselves by adjustments to suit their changing needs. For this the Hindus must first learn what a community is: must consciously accept the ideal of an unceasing activity directed towards the development in every possible way, of the physical, moral and intellectual life of each member. It must in other words feel, think and act as one whole. The theory of Hindu life so far does not accept the ideal of a Hindu community. But the practice, as we have shown, has changed with measured slowness during the last century, attaining at the present time a rapidity and momentum which could not have been anticipated. The Hindu community, still non-existent in fact has come into existence in idea. The translation of that idea in the realm of practice is the mission of present day Hinduism.

It was August Comte who emphasised the inseparable connection of the physical, intellectual and moral aspects of life with material conditions. The change in material conditions has produced in India the conception of a Hindu community, has awakened the consciousness in Hindus of all classes that they are Hindus and as a result has created equally in all classes burning resentment against the customs and laws which have unjustly stunted the growth of the Hindu peoples. Customs like untouchability which the reformers of an earlier generation recognised to be morally iniquitous have come to be regarded also as socially pernicious. The growth of the feeling of community in these matters is attested incontrovertibly by the fact that the resentment against these unsocial customs is felt with great intensity by members of all classes, not the least by the more intelligent among the Brahmins themselves. Indeed it is significant that in all the movements meant to ameliorate the miseries which arise from social institutions, it is the higher caste Hindus that have toiled and sacrificed.

When social feeling has reached that stage of awakening when injustice of every kind kindles resentment, the organisation of society through legislation becomes possible. It is the argument of this book that the translation of the idea of community from the realm of mind to the realm of activity through the creation of social institutions has now been rendered possible by the establishment of a democratic machinery of legislation. It will no doubt be pointed out that it is but little that legislation can do to reform communities: that it is the tendency of bureaucracy to exaggerate the importance of the part played by legislation in matters affecting the ethical life of people. It is no doubt true that legislation by itself can achieve little: but the important difference is this. Where the social conscience has already come to believe in the necessity of change, legislation can give to such changes, direction, form and what is more, continuity. It is also true that the experience of societies changed all at once by law is not sufficient to warrant a faith in its ability to change human nature. Such societies have relapsed generally to their bad old ways when the authority of the state has weakened. But equally true it is that continuous legislative activity consolidating the social development of the people has been one of the most determining factors of history. Hindu law itself, was no more than the consolidation of the social feeling of the time when it was codified; and it is undoubtedly that law that has shaped Hindu life. The legislation that can save the Hindus is the further consolidation of the progress of the Hindu mind by the modification of the laws in terms of our present beliefs.

Further, though the influence of innovating legislation may be impermanent, the immeasurable power of institutions over human character will be readily accepted. The suitable and timely modification of institutions has been one of the primary duties of all self-governing communities. As we have emphasised the immobility of Hinduism arose not from a lack of realisation of the power of institutions but from the absence of machinery to modify and renovate them. Even the most rigidly conservative of human organisations, the Roman Catholic Church, has at all times had a machinery for incorporating the changes which are found necessary into its own system. The Ecumenical Councils, the Curia and the pontificate itself provide the machinery for such constant modification. While recognizing the limitations of legislative authority, it is essential to emphasise its aspect as the realising force of social ideas which have already received wide acceptance. Whether that authority is derived through a State or a Church is of minor matter. What is important is that unless the sanction of law is behind social changes, every effort towards reform will only lead to further chaos. In fact the social anarchy of Hinduism is as much due to unregulated "reform" which tended to be local and sectional, as to disintegration.

The organisation of society through initiative from the centre and established through the compelling power of dictatorial authority has been the most outstanding feature of the present day. The power of institutions to shape human mind is the basic doctrine of the fascist as of the communist States. But the dictatorship whether of the proletariat or of the totalitarians looks upon the complex powers of the State not as a machinery for bringing social institutions in step with social ideas but of changing society according to a particular theory. How far such dictatorships exaggerate the power of legislation to instil new ideas in the people is yet to be known. But it is a far cry from the abolition of God by legislation, to the modification of existing institutions by the incorporation by law of accepted social ideas.

In asking for the renovation of social energies the Hindus do not deny their past or question the wisdom of their ancestors.